First published 2019
by KingFisher Publishing Ltd
NZBN: 9429046616180

Copyright © 2019 KingFisher Publishing Ltd

All rights reserved. No part of this publication may be reproduced, stored in a retrival systems, or transmitted in any form or by any means electronic, mechanical, photocopying, recording, or otherwise, without the prior written consent of the copyright owner.

ISBN: 978-0-473-48235-0
Published in Christchurch, Aotearoa

www.kingfisherpublishing.com

Dream Big. Work Hard. Make it Happen.
THERESE FISHER

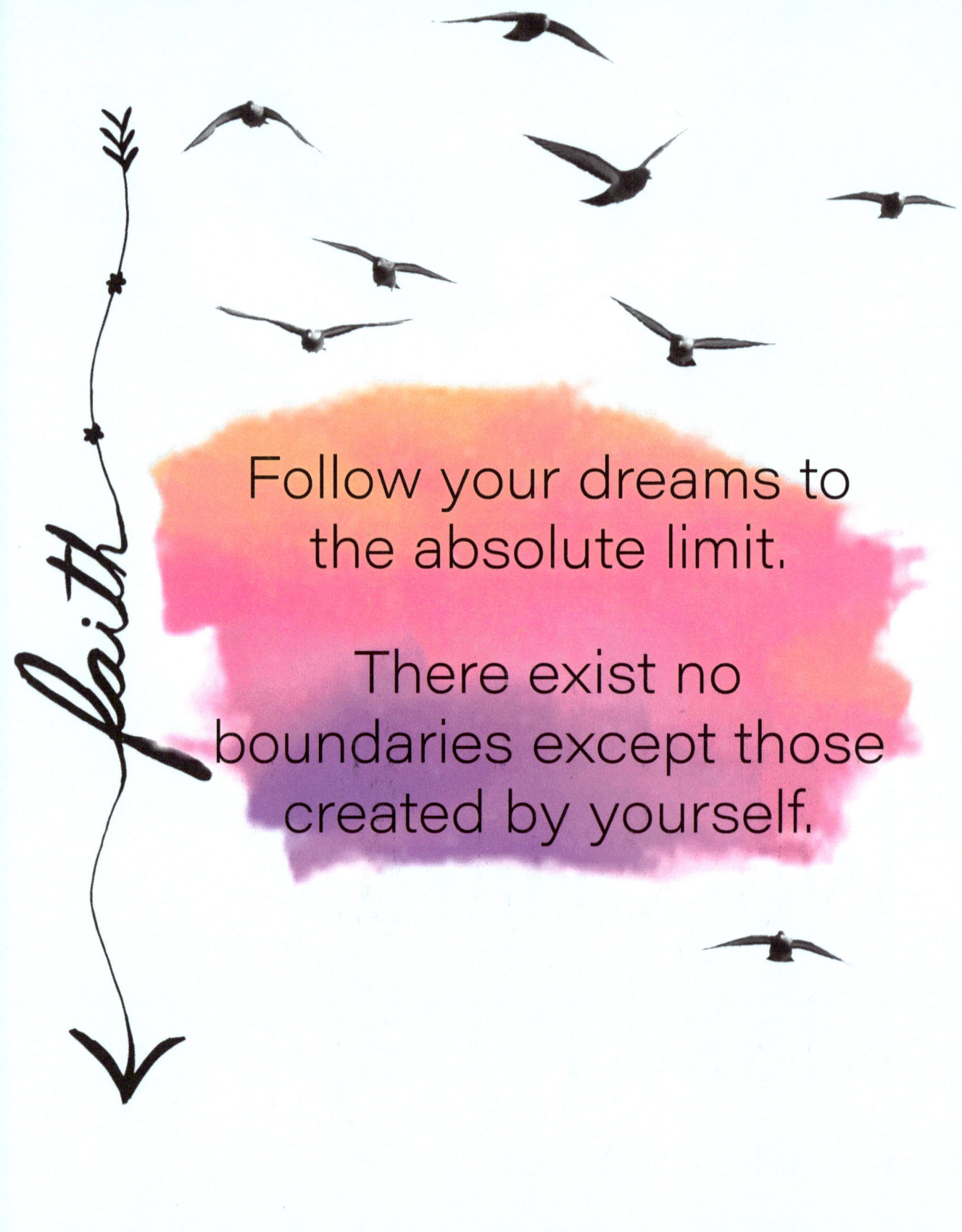

Purpose
Fuels
Passion

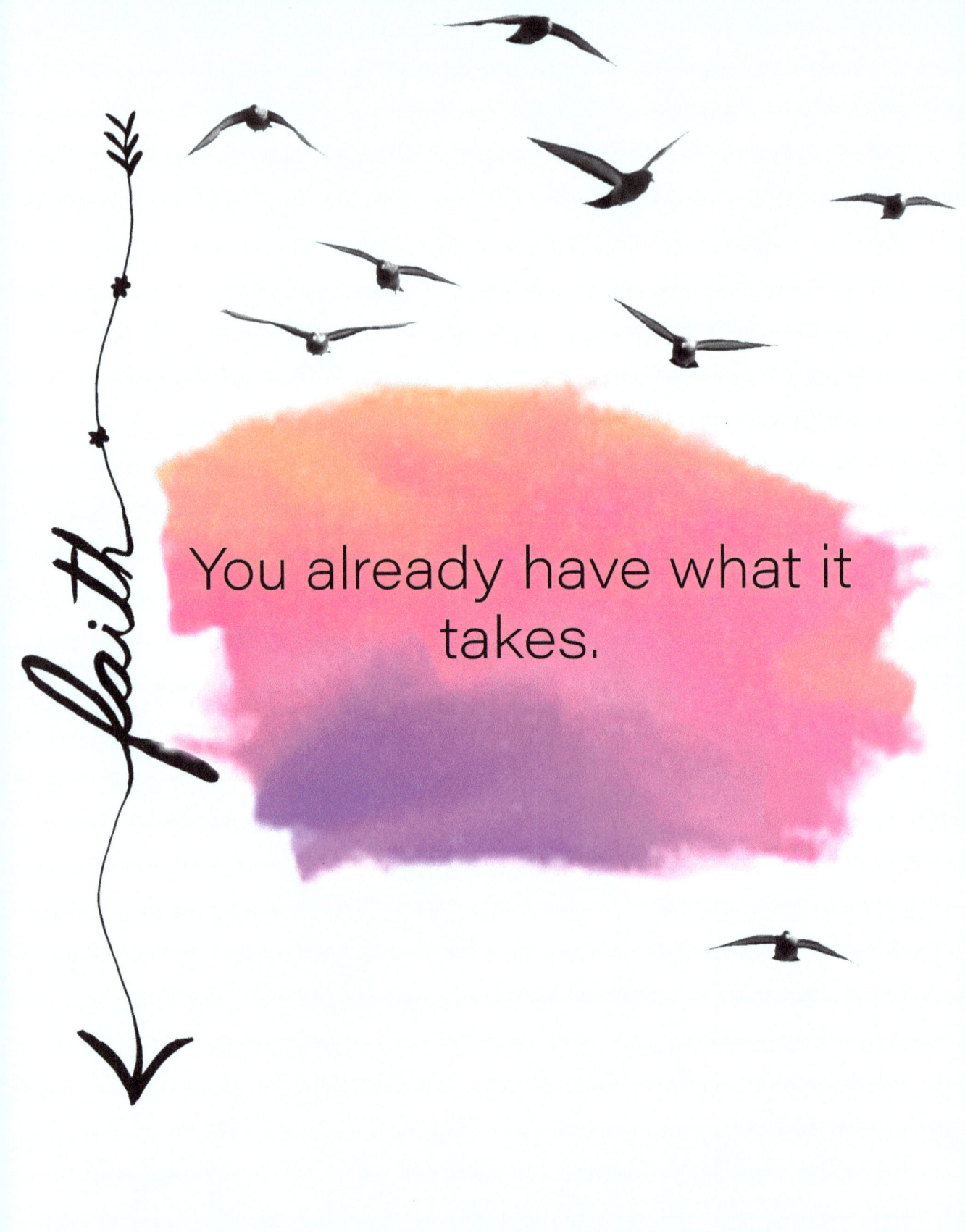

There is no failure.
You either win or you learn

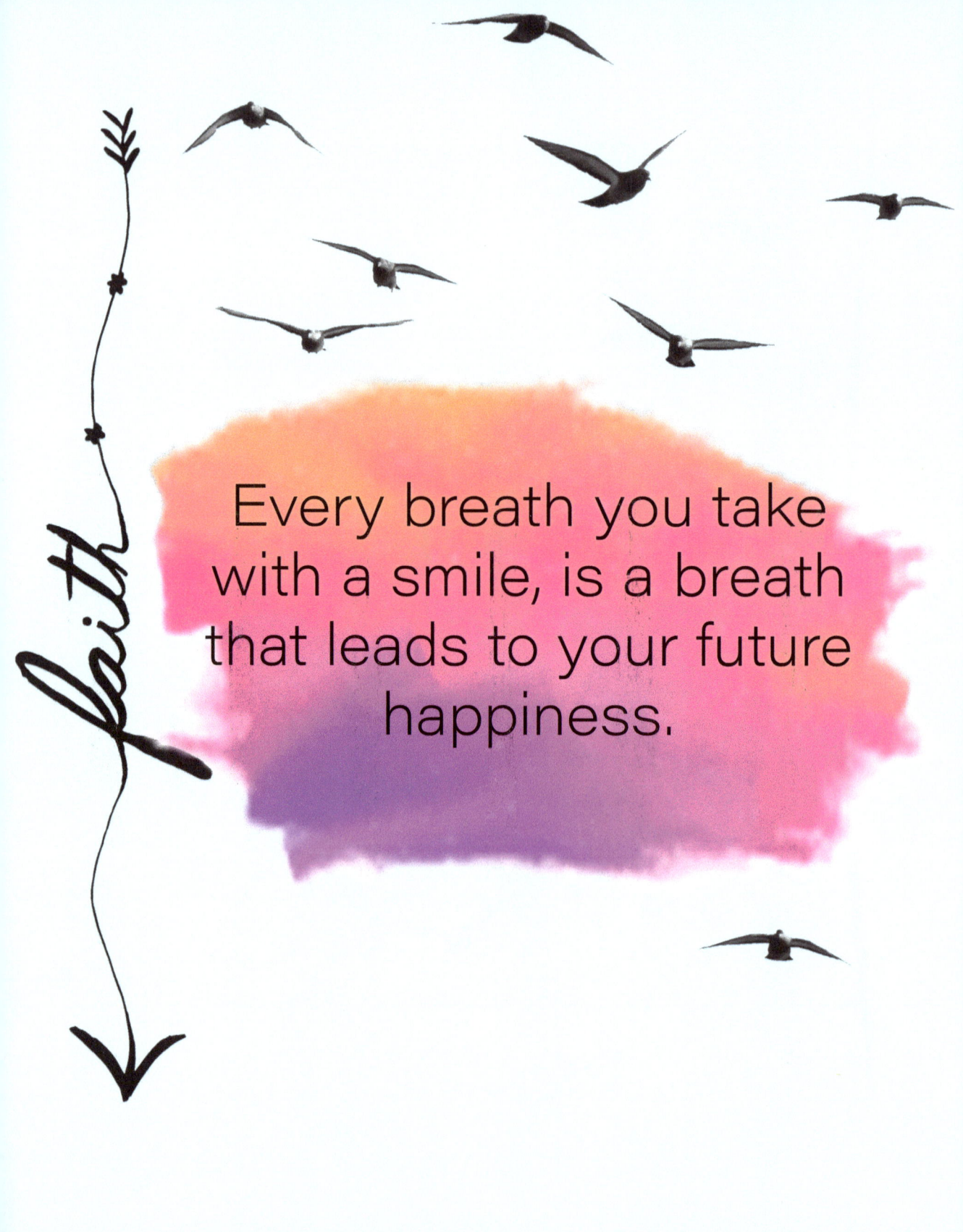

Be not afraid.
God is with
you always.

Your heart knows the way.

Be fearless
in the pursuit
of that which sets
your soul on fire

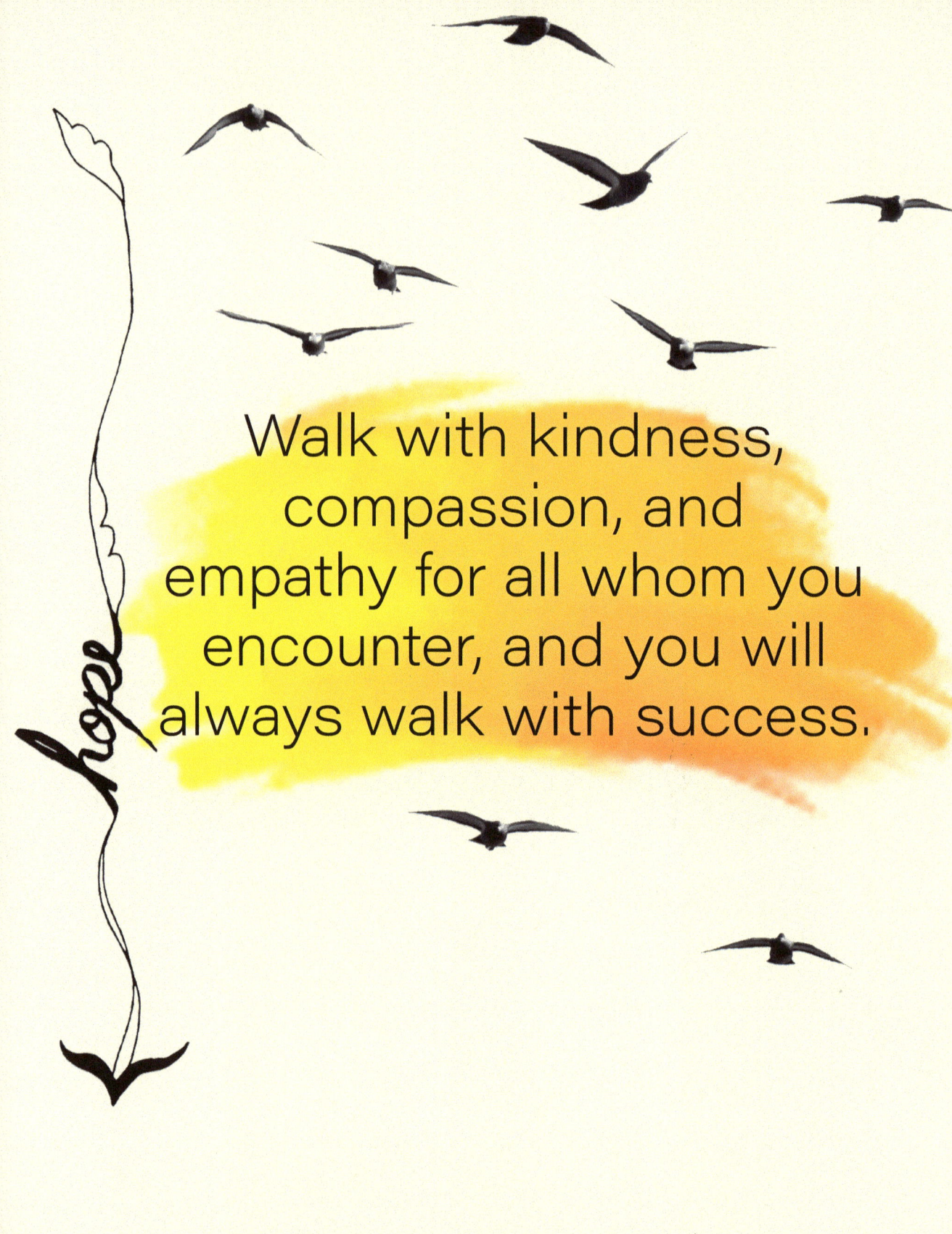

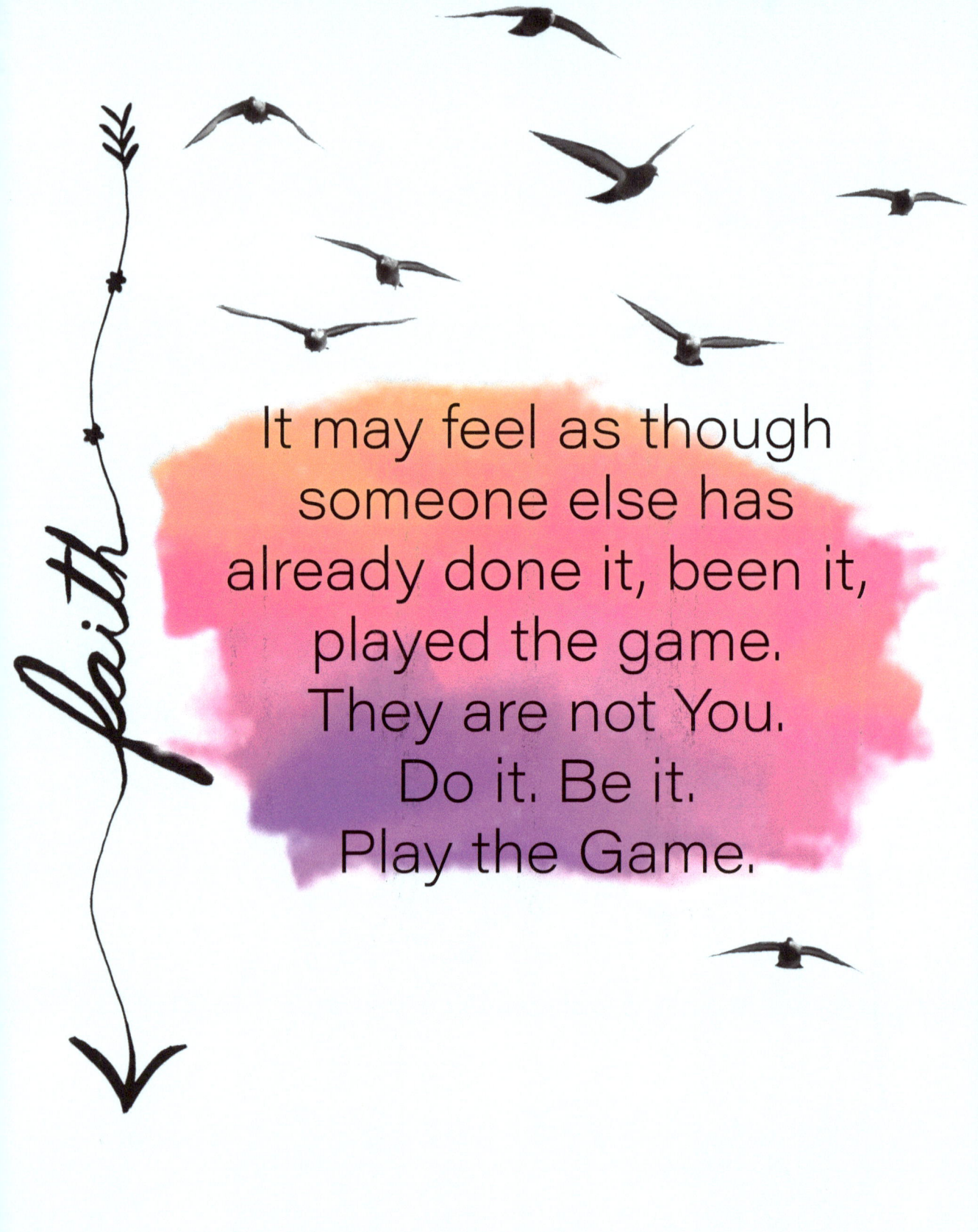

Live your best life every day.

SMILE

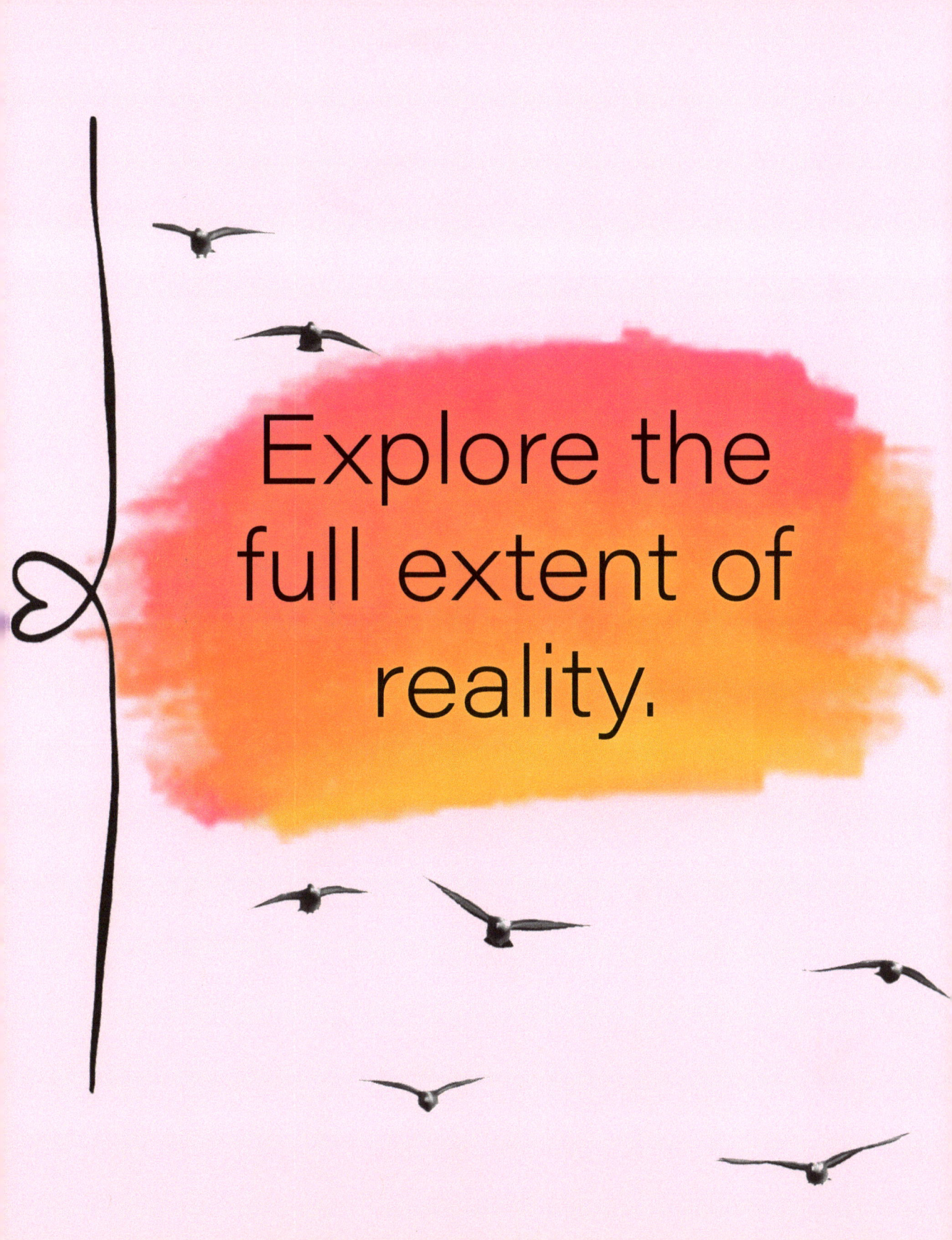

Do the small things in a great way.

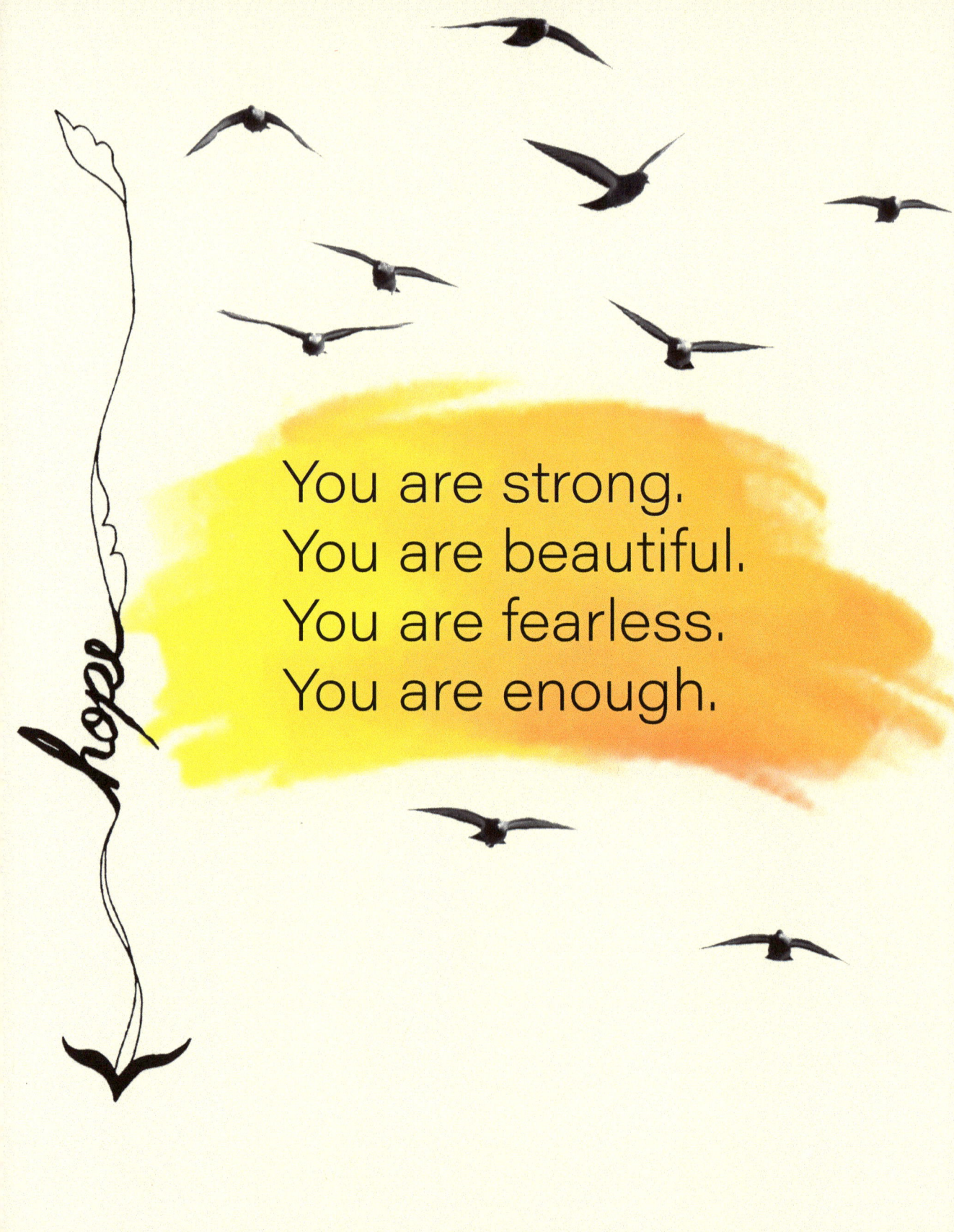

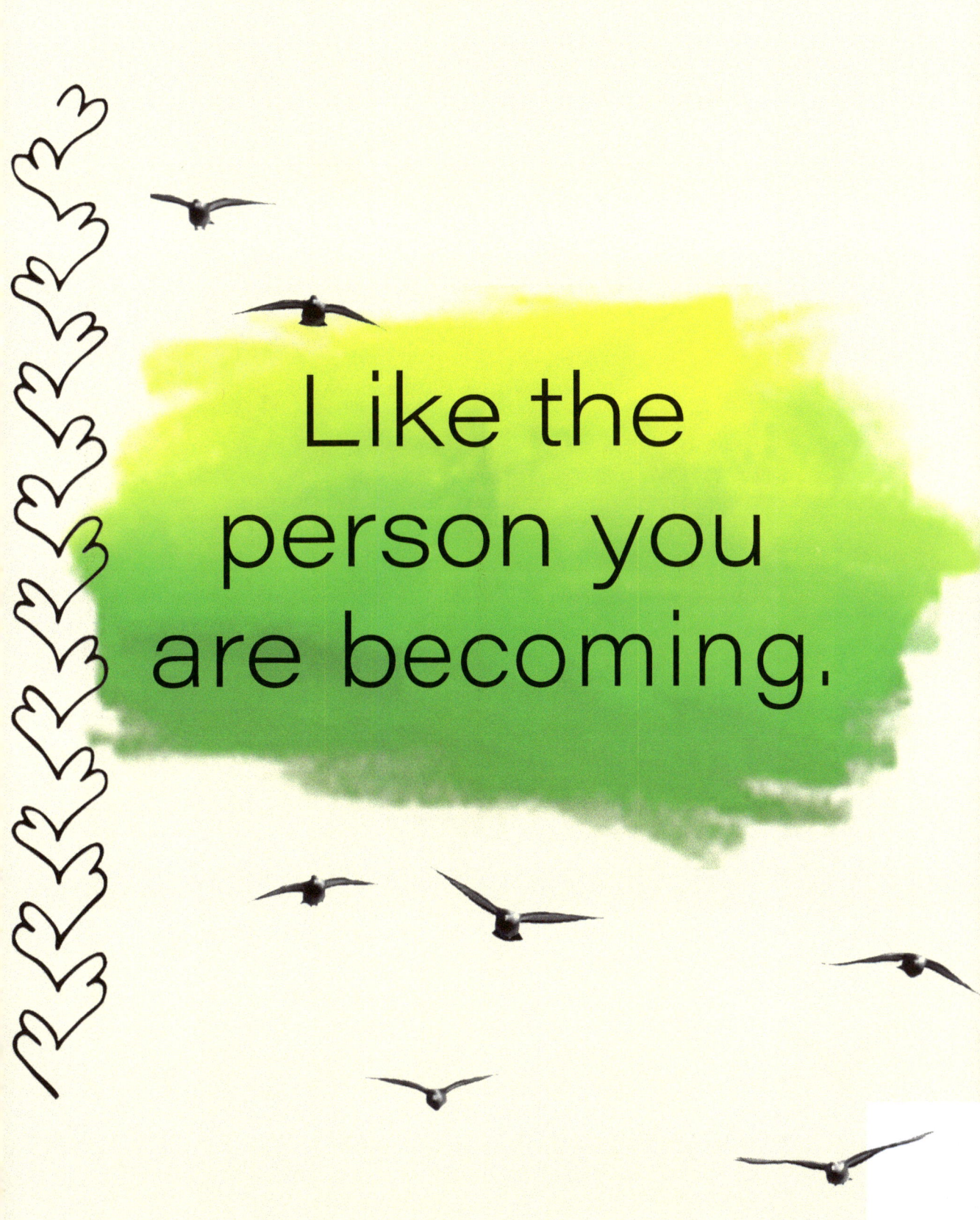

BE
-YOU-
-TIFUL

Don't let your fear decide your future.

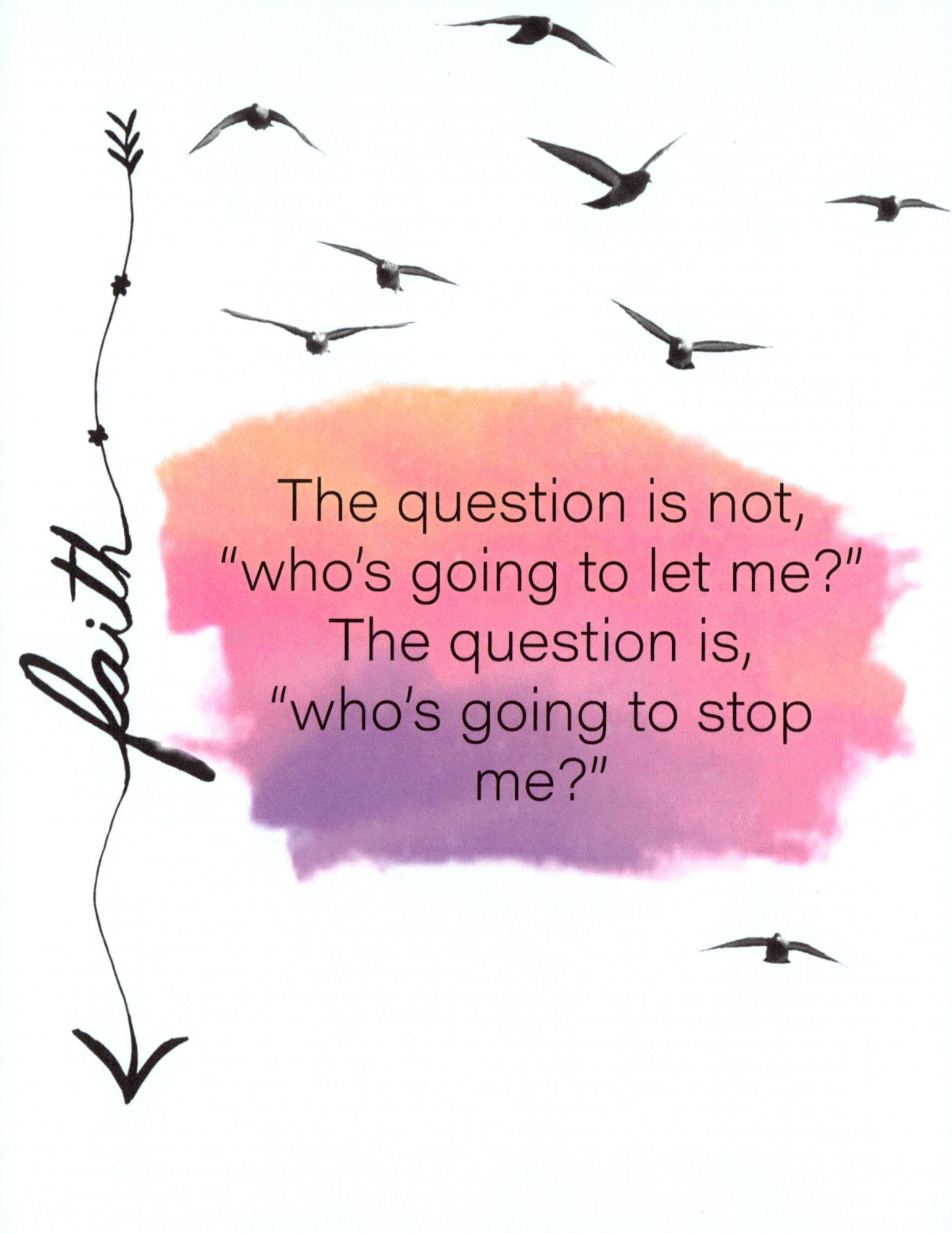

If you obey all the rules, you miss all the fun.

You can
and
You will

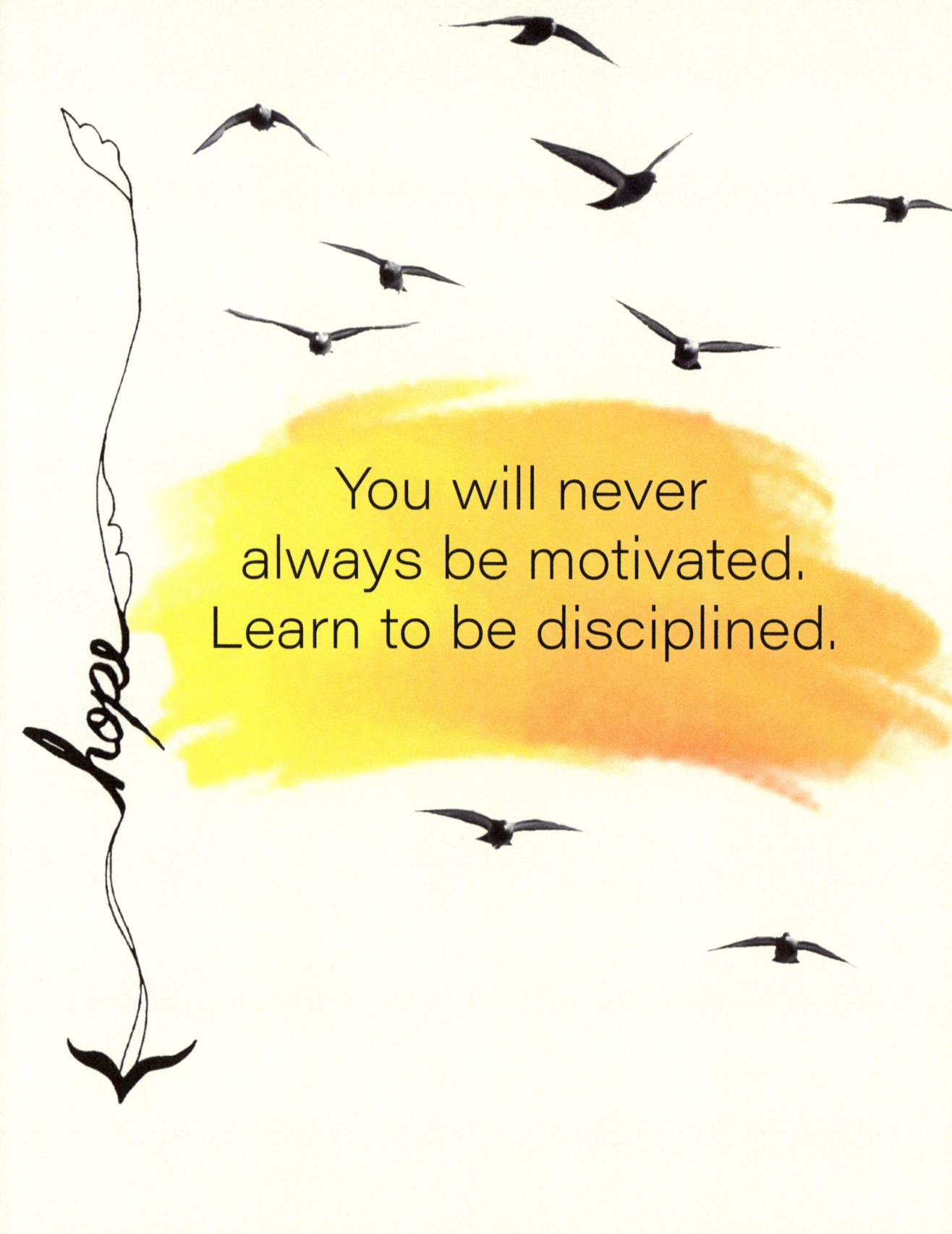

Don't busy.
Be productive.

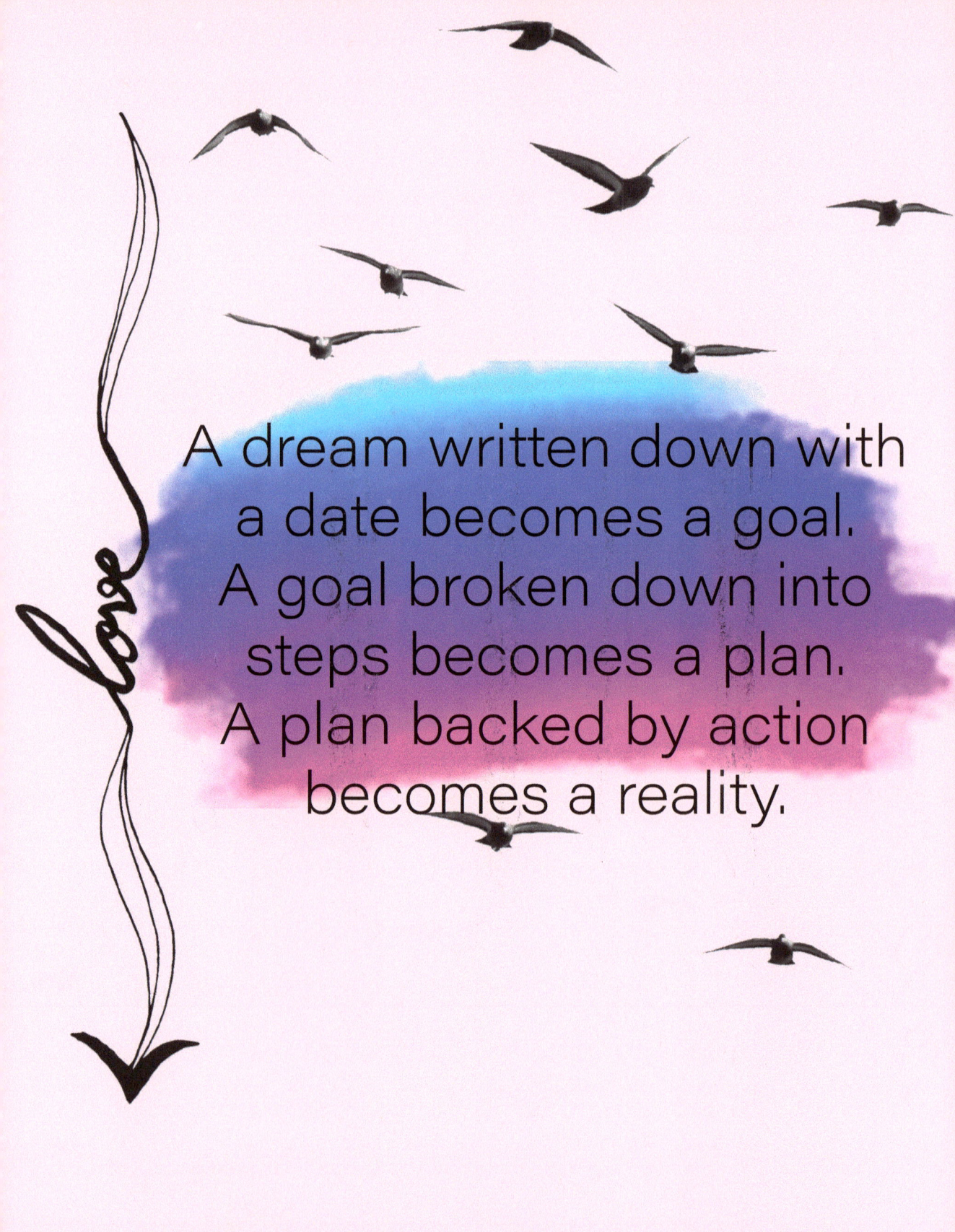

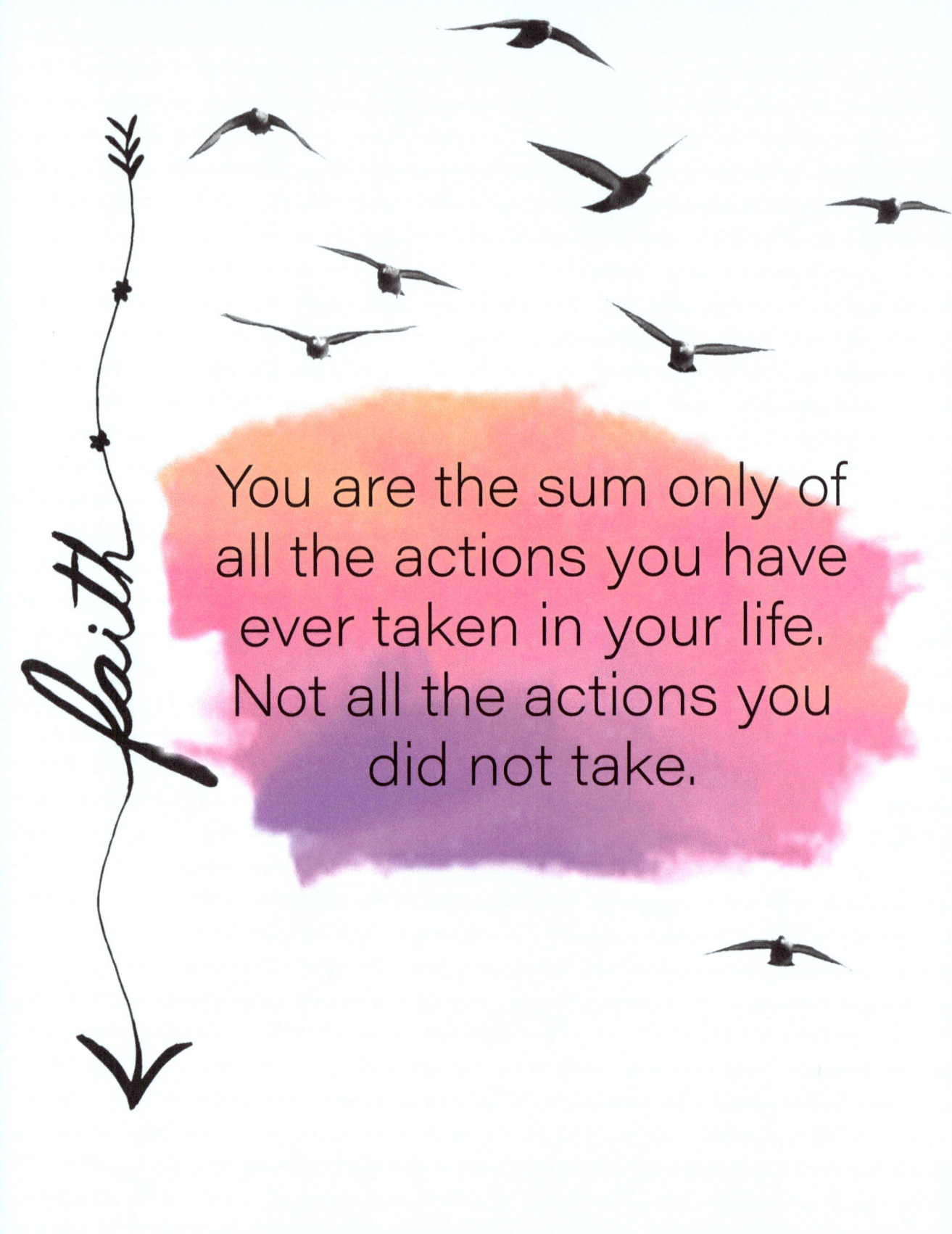

Realise the depth of your potential.

Build your own castle.

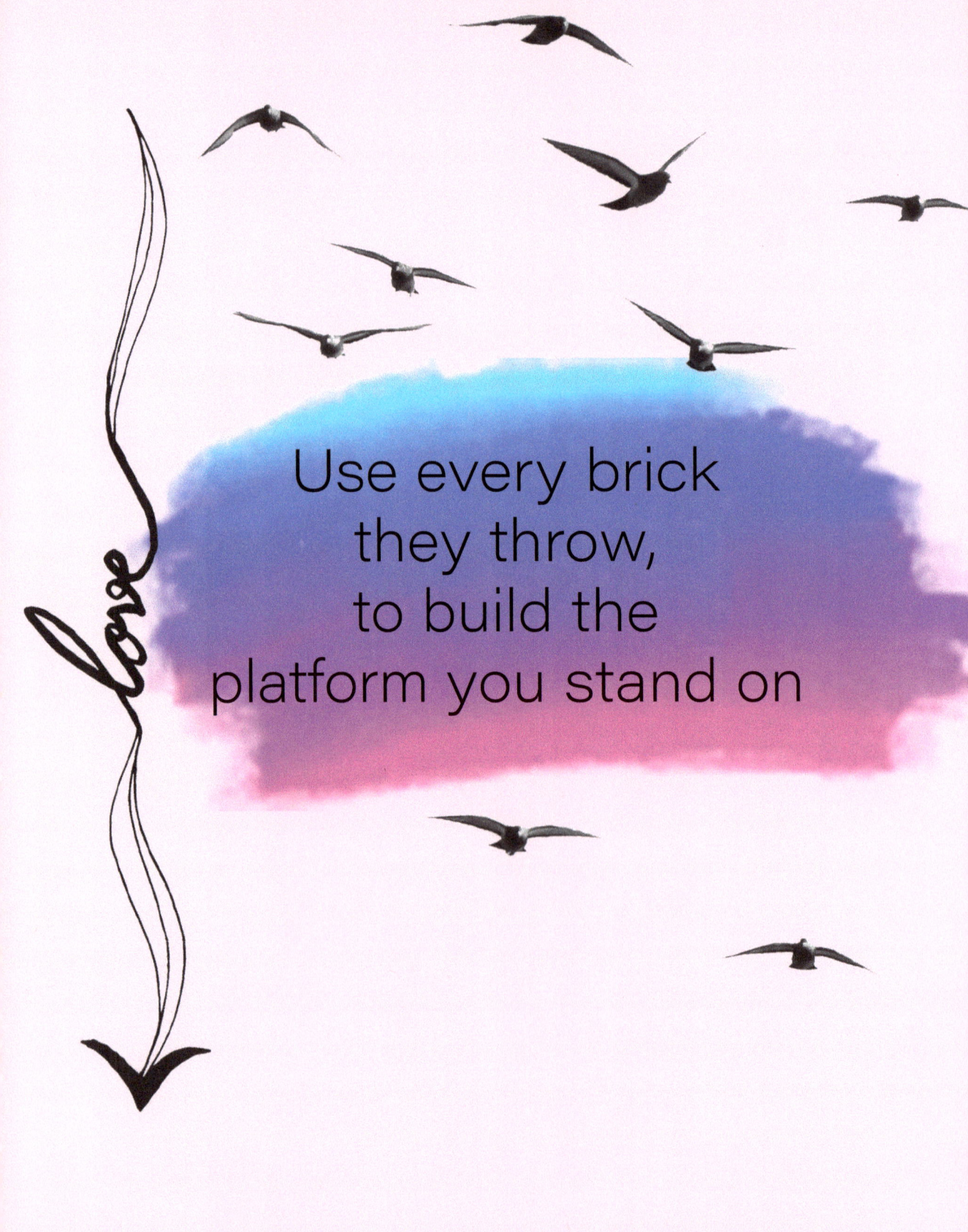

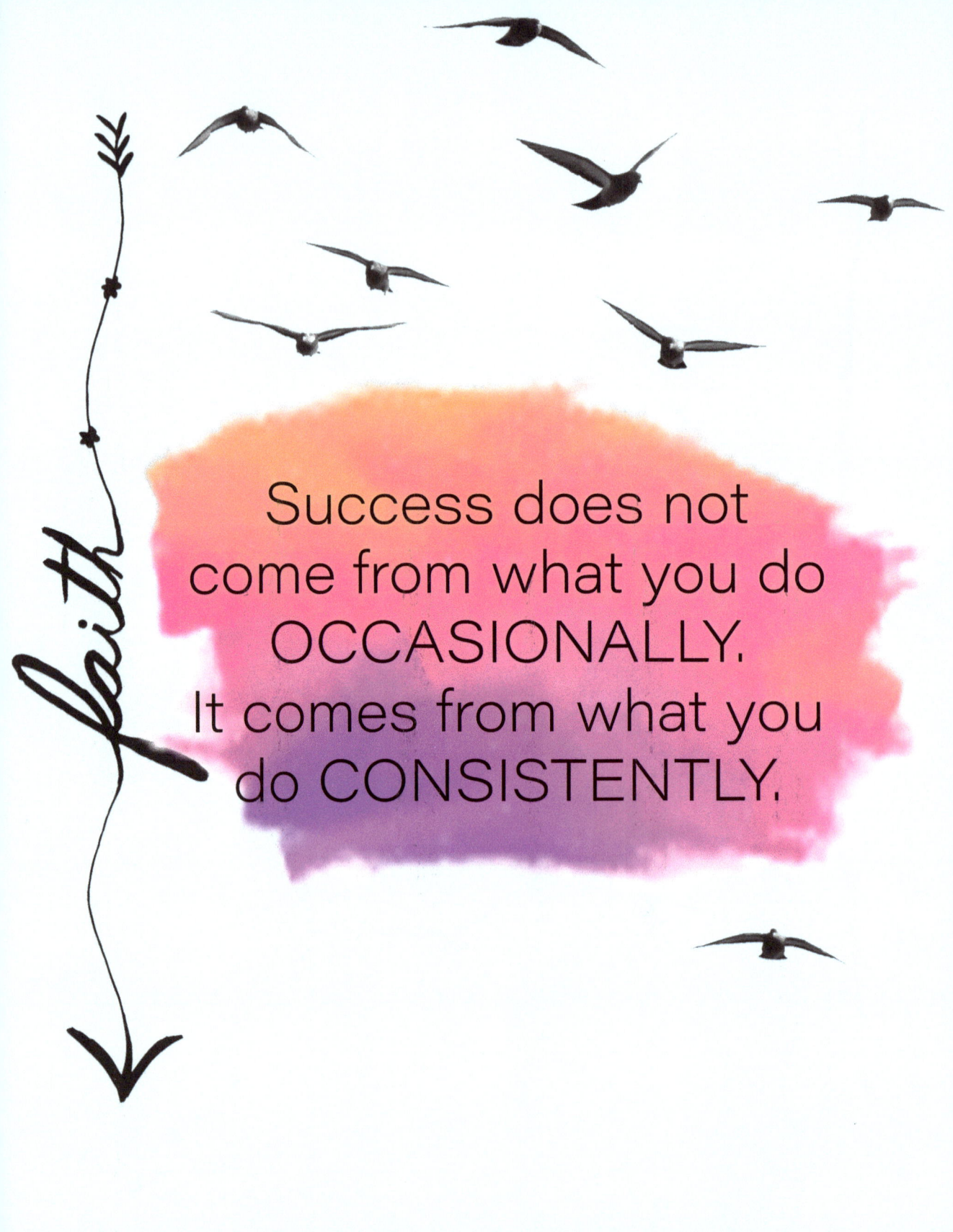

You are ready NOW.
Take the leap.

Don't just tell people your dreams. Show them.

Carpe Diem!

Change 'Why Me' to 'Try Me.'

Start TODAY.

If opportunity doesn't knock, build the door.

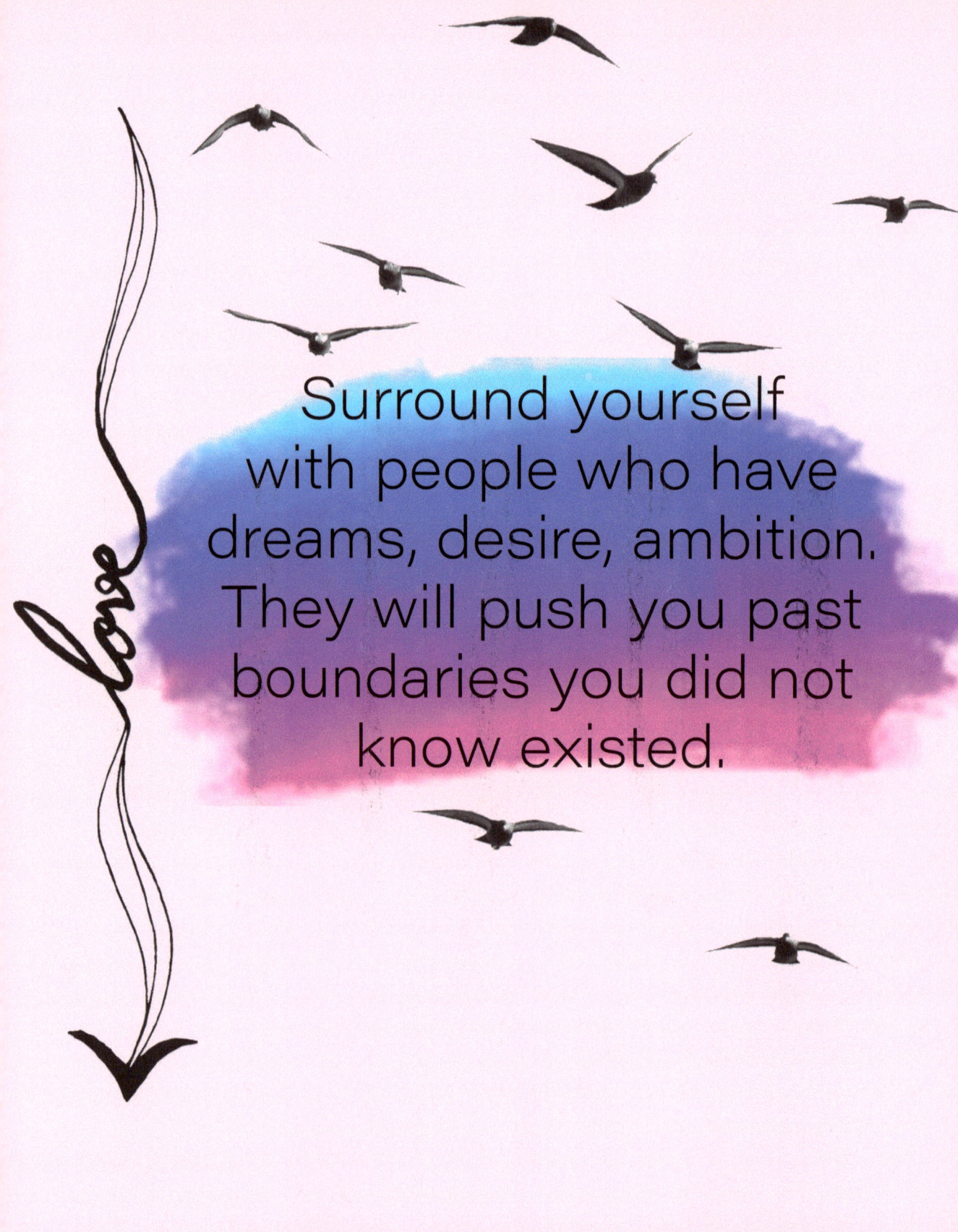

Do the thing.

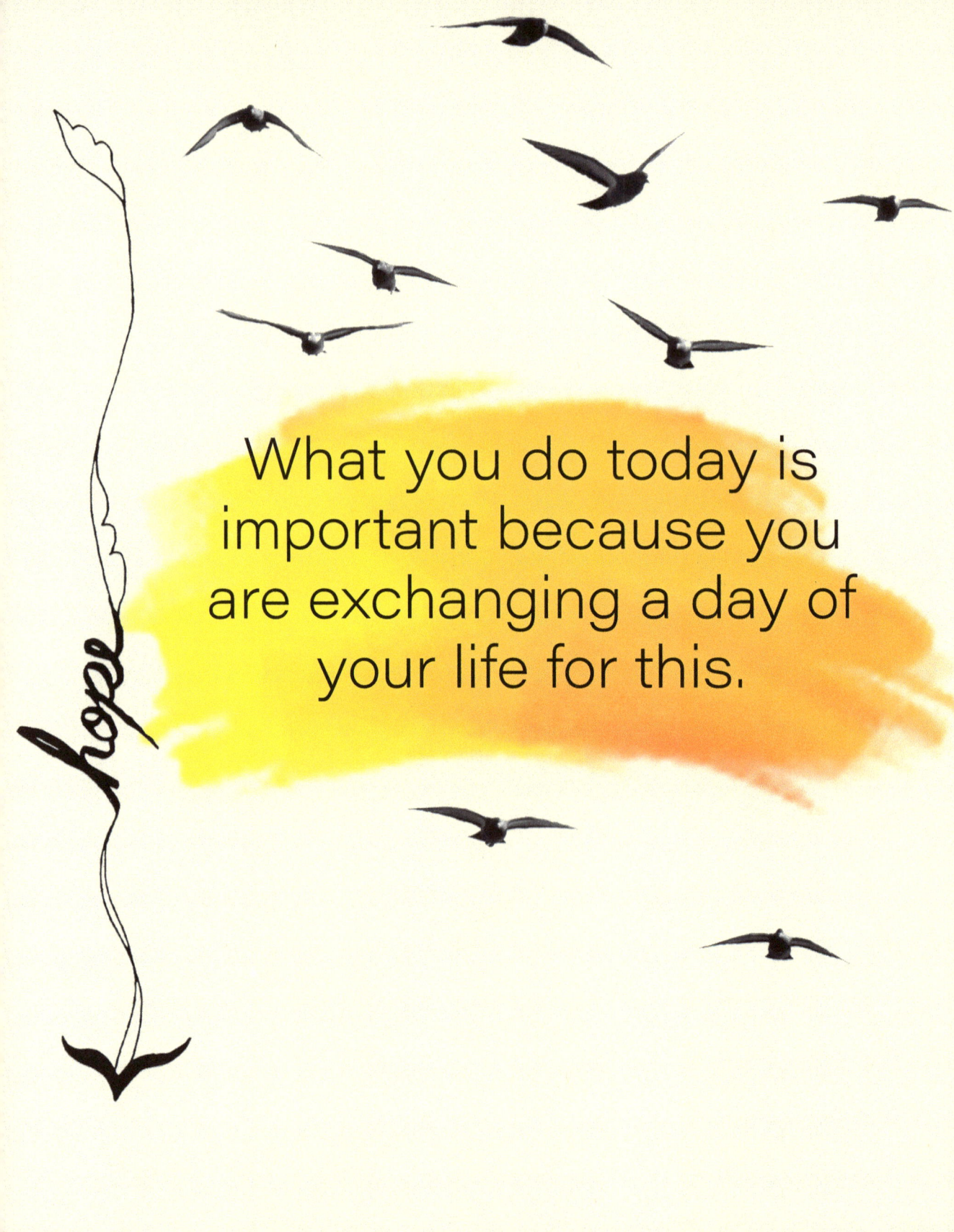

Make your passion, your paycheck.

The best time for a new start is now.

Create the opportunity you are waiting for.

Make today a great day!

If you stumble, make it part of the dance.

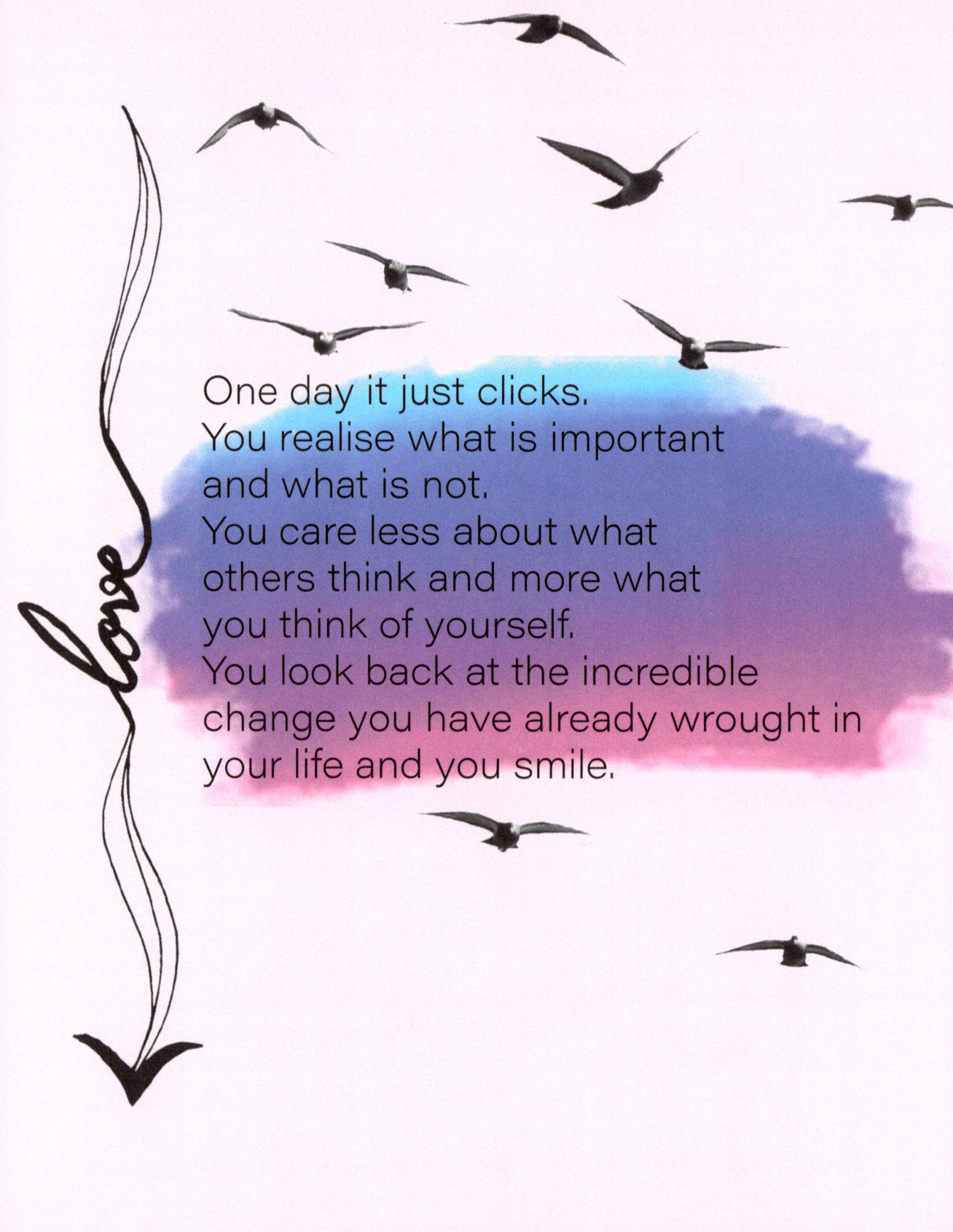

One day it just clicks.
You realise what is important
and what is not.
You care less about what
others think and more what
you think of yourself.
You look back at the incredible
change you have already wrought in
your life and you smile.

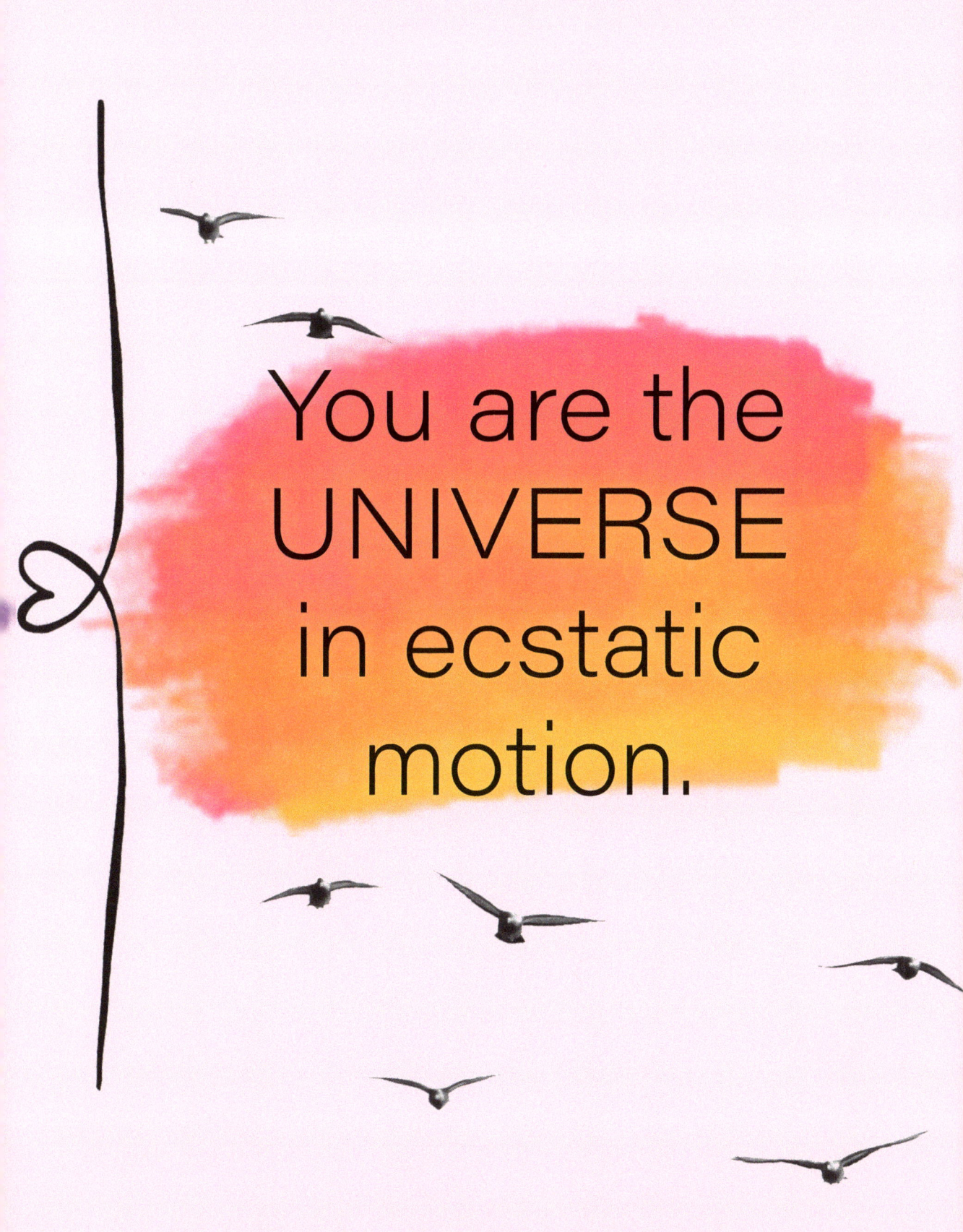

Love the life you live.

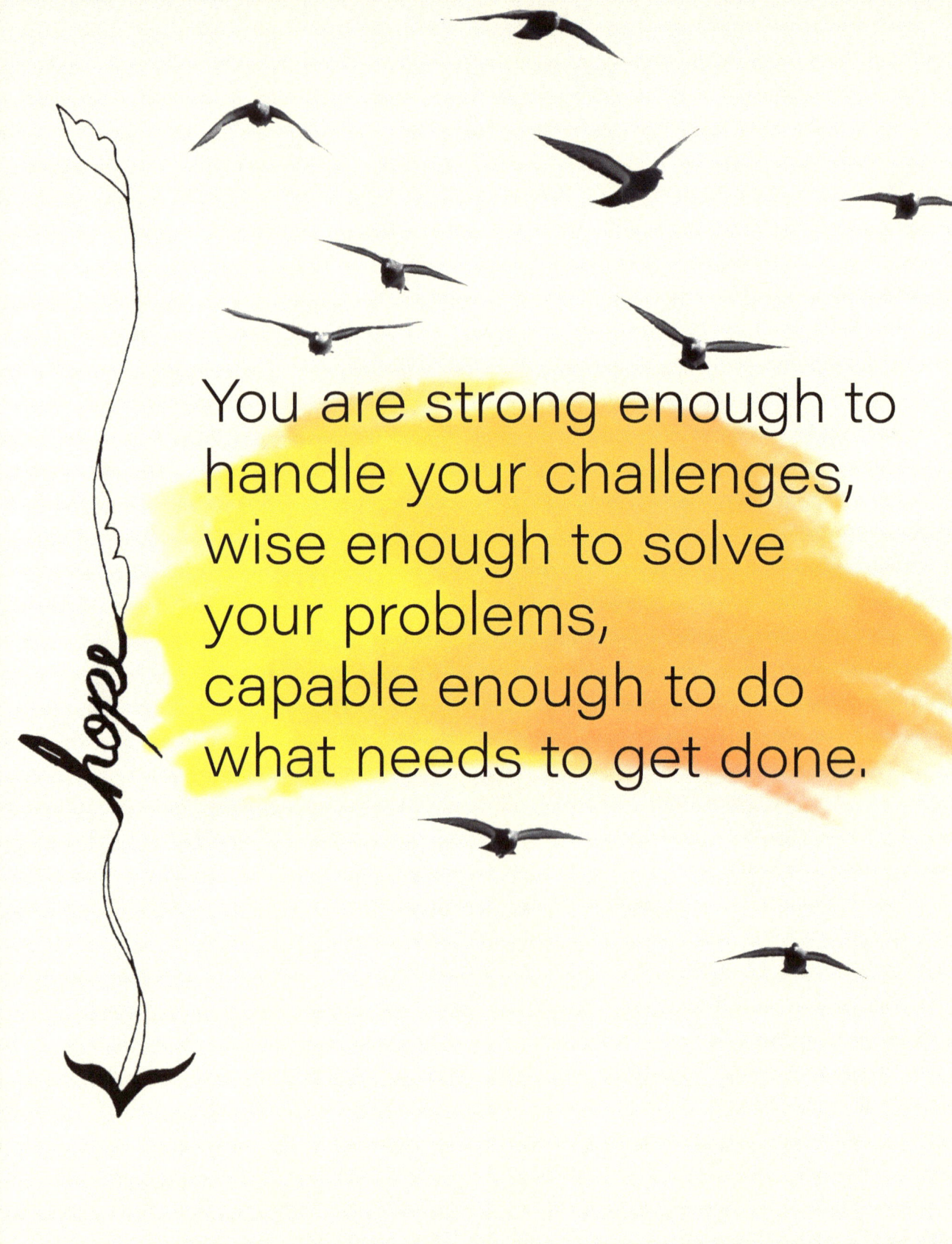

YOU ARE ENOUGH

Write a check to your future self.

You only fail when you stop trying.

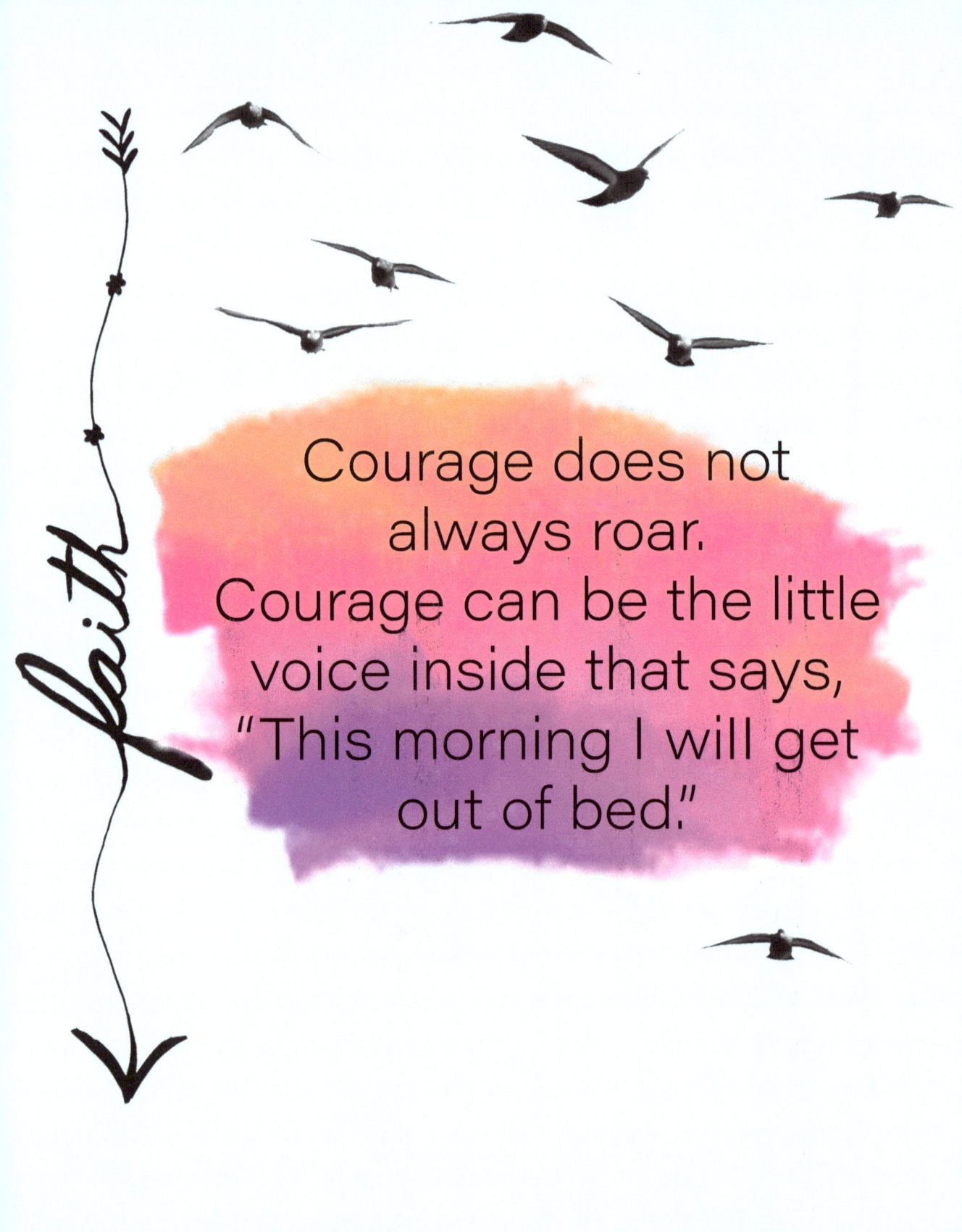

You can.
You should.
You will.

Say YES to new adventures.

Never stop looking up.

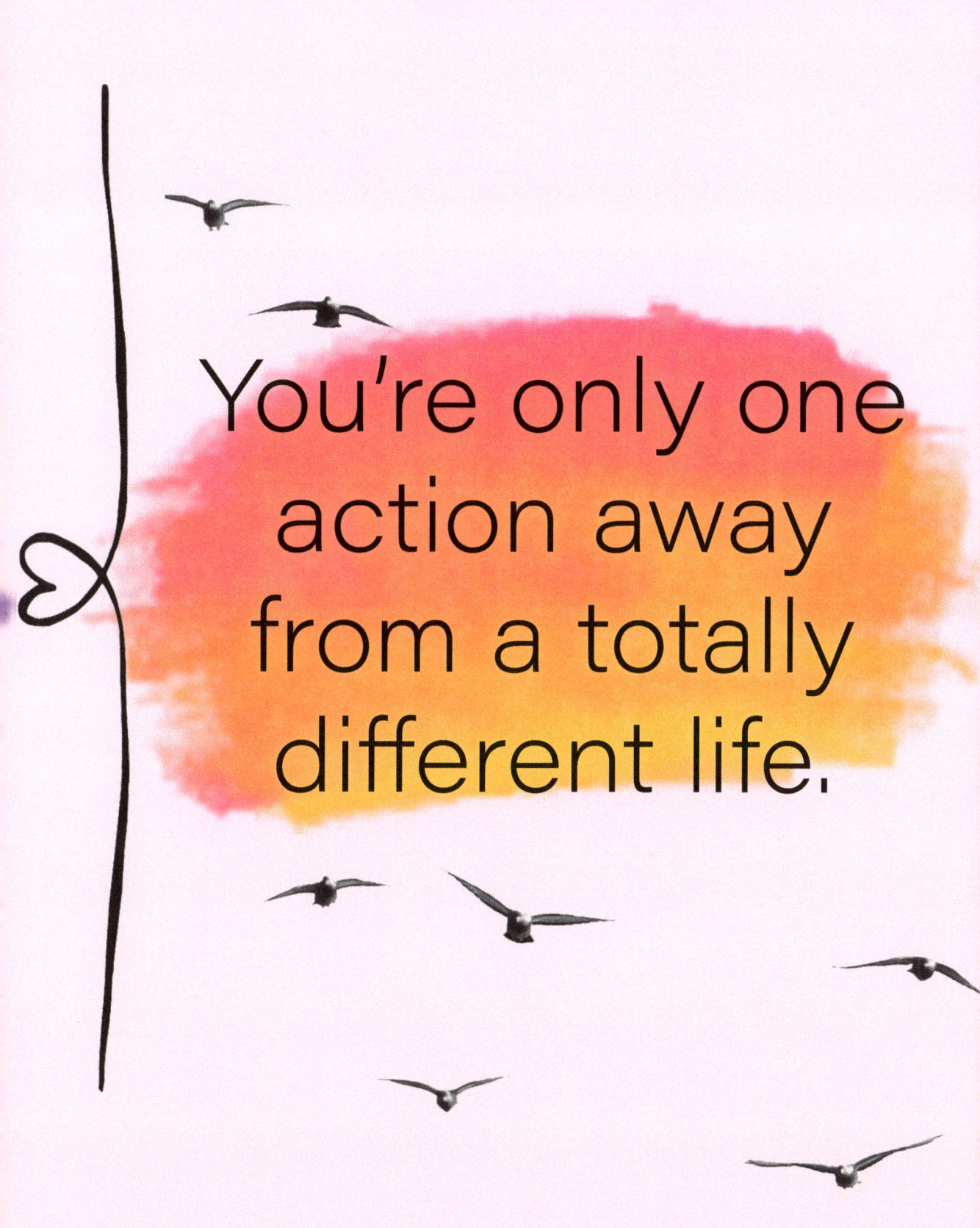

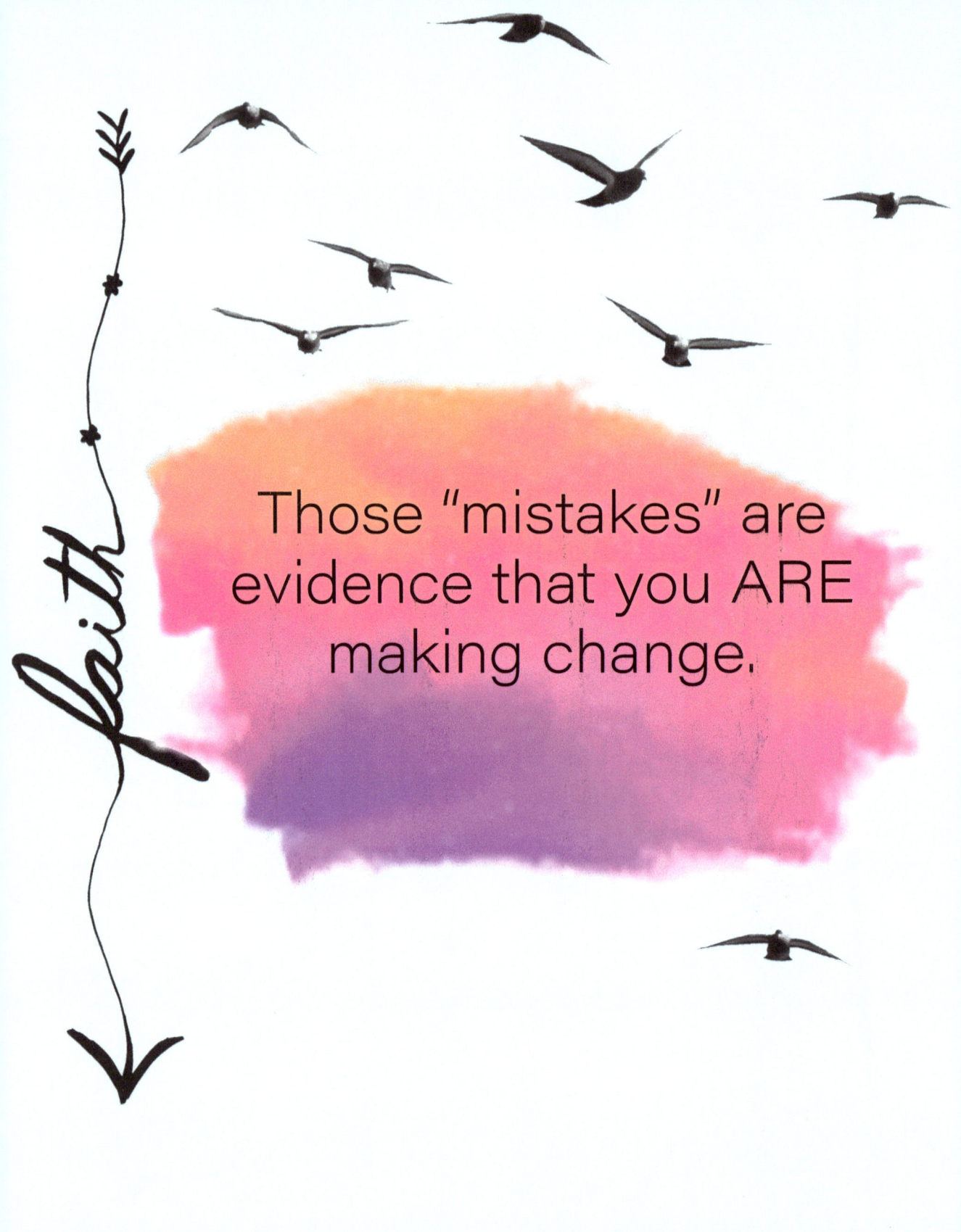

Grow through AROHA.

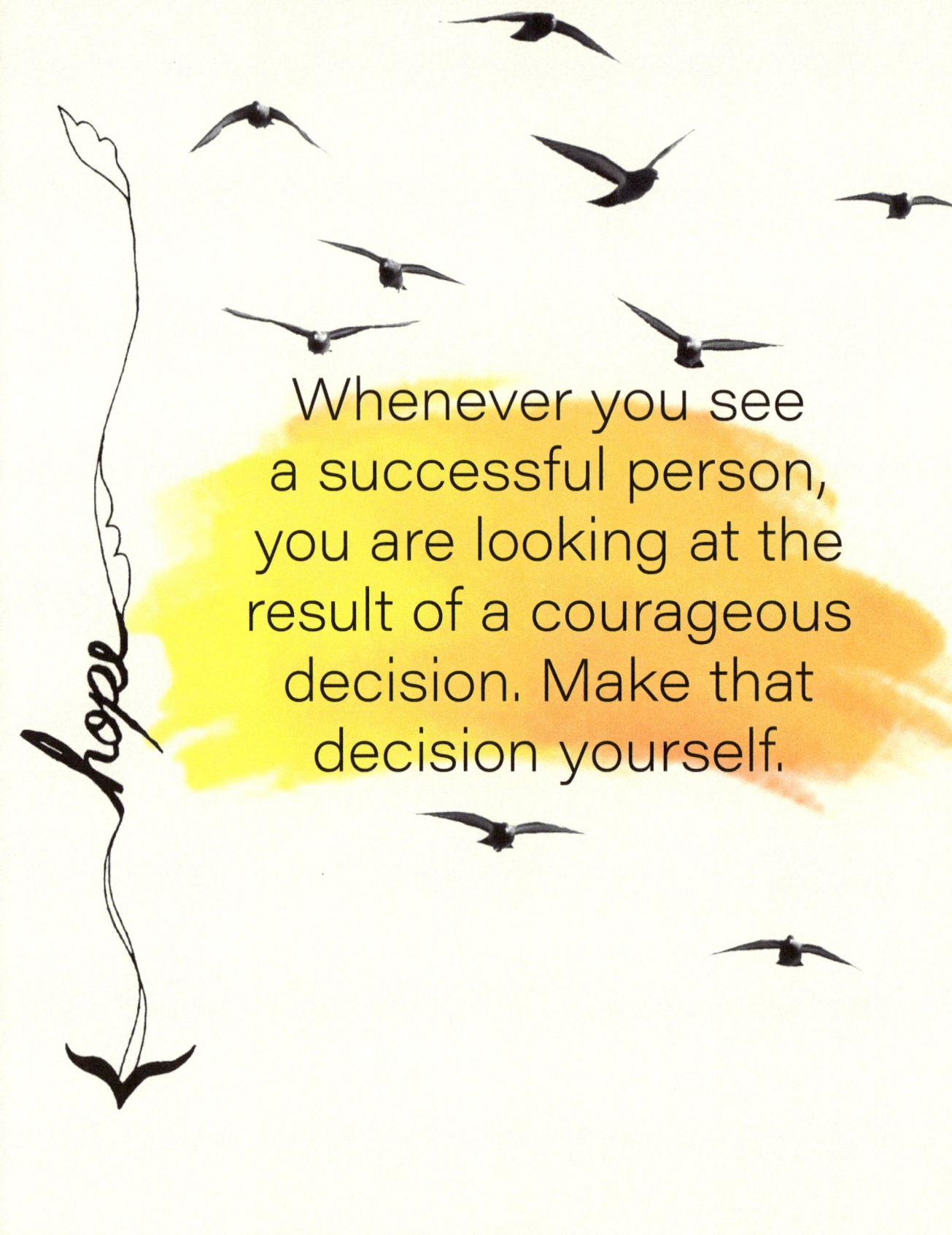

You are terrific.

JUST
DO
IT

EMBRACE CHANGE

You cannot speak words of failure and defeat and expect a life of success and victory.

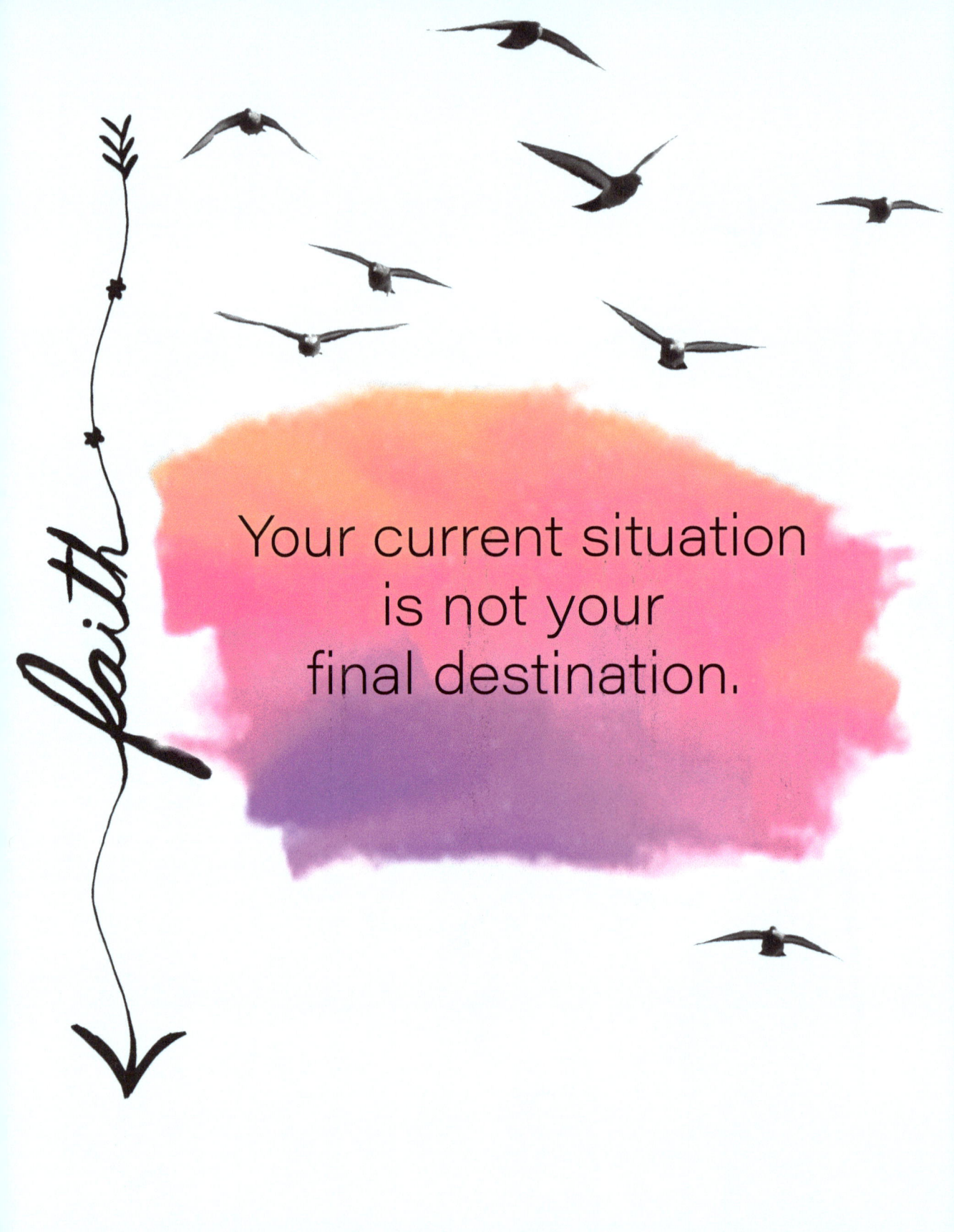

Whatever you are, be the best.

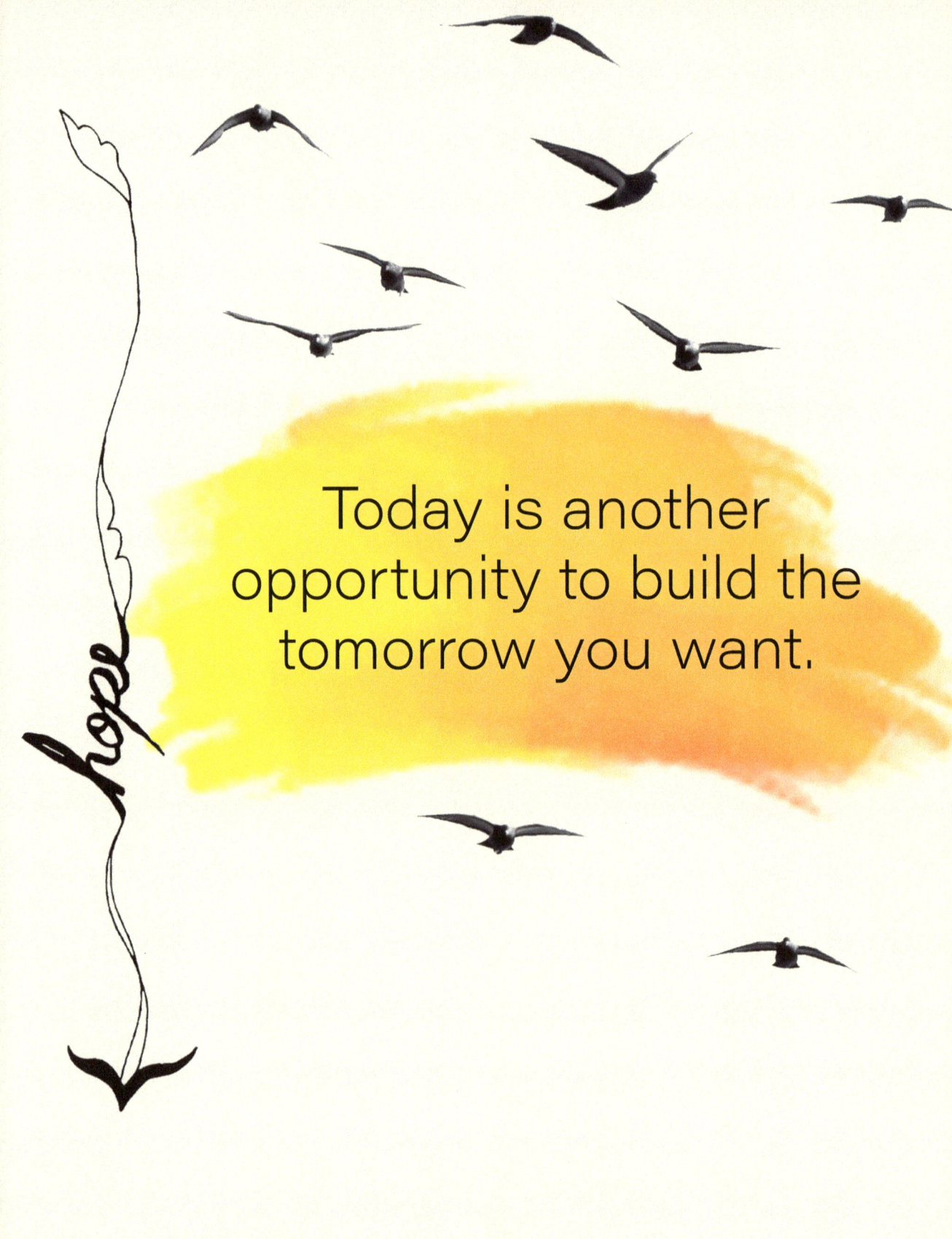

Take the GOOD from every day

Don't stop until you are PROUD.

LIVE FOR LIFE

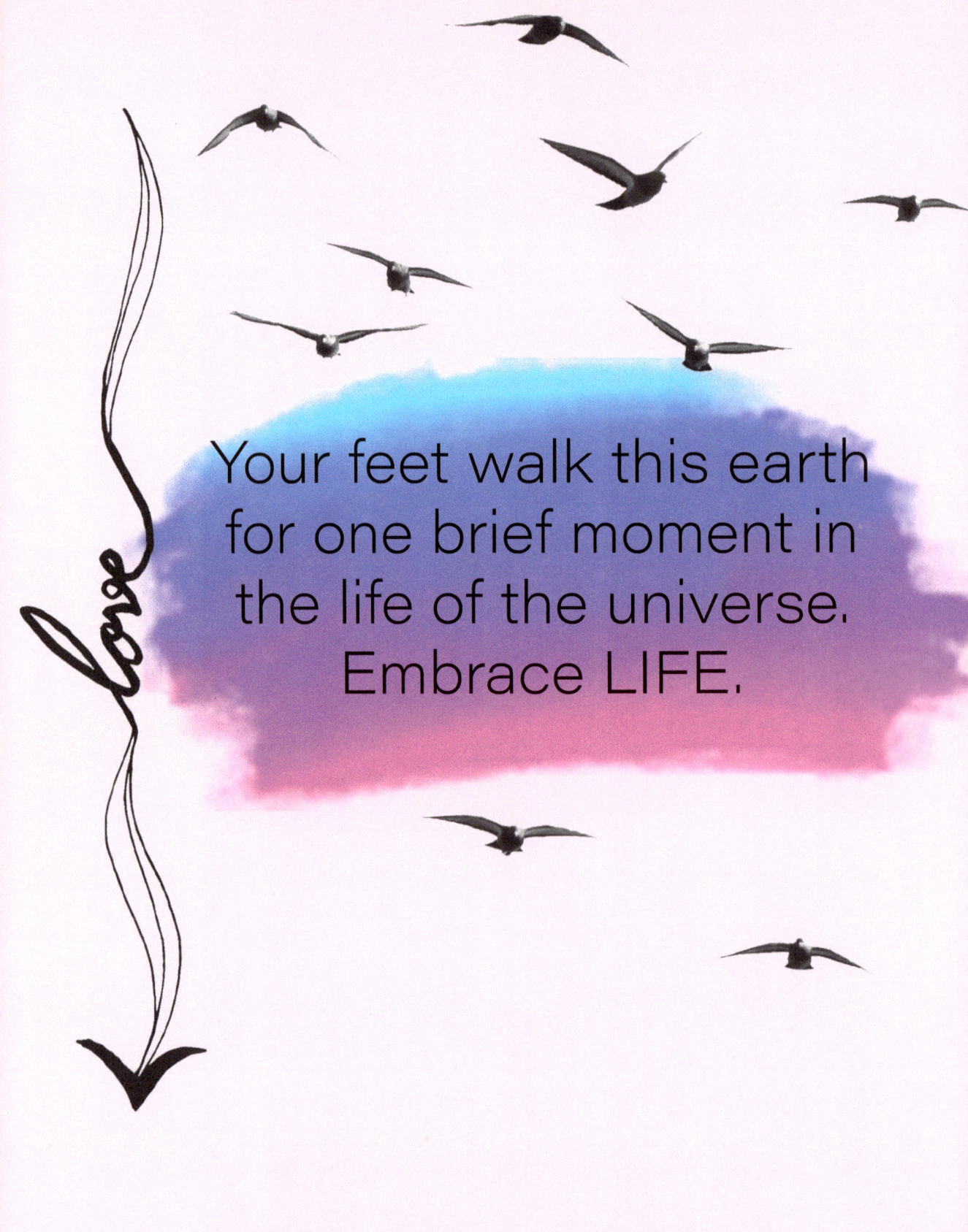

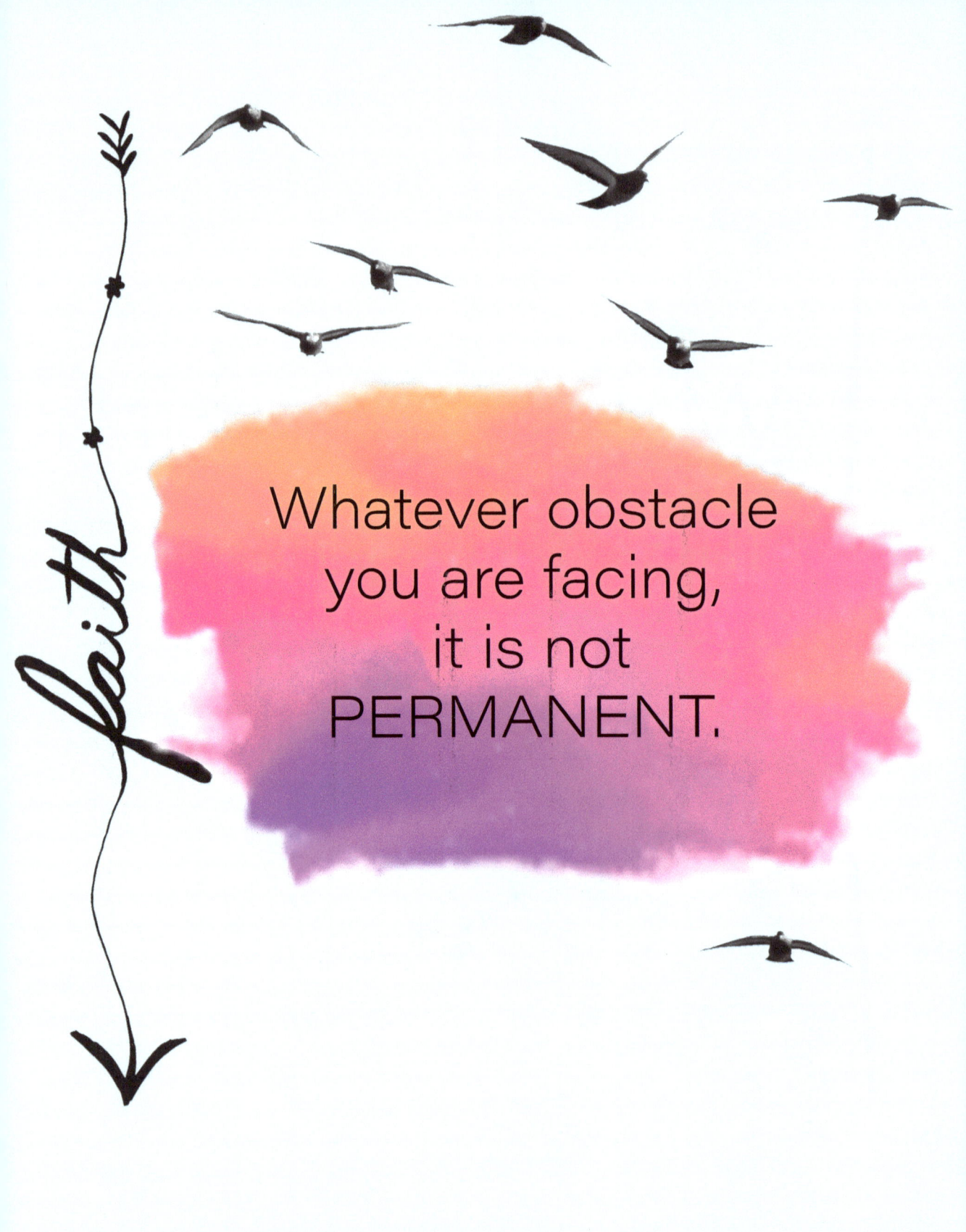

I wish you peace in all things.

Be true to yourself

Lift up
your heart

All you ever have is NOW.

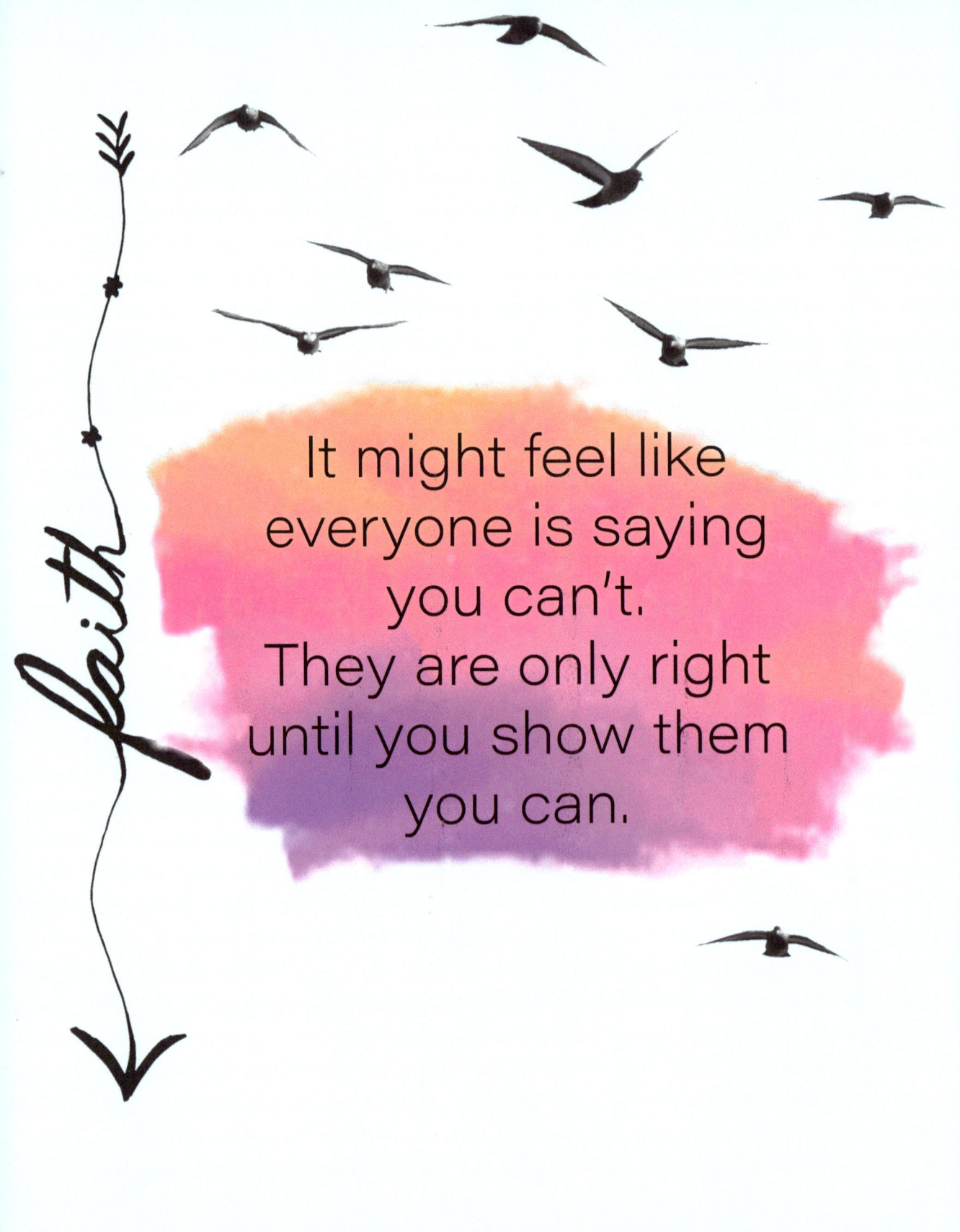

I believe in YOU